Top Dog

The Dalmatian

by William R. Sanford and Carl R. Green

CRESTWOOD HOUSE

New York

CIP
LIBRARY OF CONGRESS CATALOGING IN PUBLICATION DATA

Sanford, William R. (William Reynolds)
Dalmatian

(Top dog)
Includes index.
SUMMARY: Discusses the history, physical characteristics, care, and breeding of this dog known for its distinctive spots.
1. Dalmatian dog — Juvenile literature. [1. Dalmatian dog. 2. Dogs.] I. Green, Carl R. II. Title. III. Series: Sanford, William R. (William Reynolds), Top dog.
SF429.D3S36   1989   636.7'2 — dc20   89-31107
ISBN 0-89686-449-9

PHOTO CREDITS
Cover: Reynolds Photography: Larry Reynolds
Cheryl Steinmetz: 4, 7, 12, 21, 25, 31, 35, 36, 40
Reynolds Photography: (Larry Reynolds) 11, 23
Photo Researchers, Inc.: (Mary Eleanor Browning) 14
Animals Animals: (Frank Roche) 19; (Robert Pearcy) 42, 44

Macmillan Publishing Company
866 Third Avenue
New York, NY 10022
Collier Macmillan Canada, Inc.

CRESTWOOD HOUSE
Produced by Carnival Enterprises

Printed in the United States of America

First Edition

10 9 8 7 6 5 4 3 2 1

TABLE OF CONTENTS

FOR MORE INFORMATION

For more information about dalmatians, write to:

American Kennel Club
51 Madison Avenue
New York, NY 10010

Dalmatian Club of America, Inc.
325 Old Mill Spring Road
Route 3
Jonesborough, TN 37659

DOTTIE SAVES THE DAY

Dottie was chewing on her favorite rawhide bone. The Dalmatian didn't know she would soon be starring on television. She didn't even care. Her world started and stopped with ten-year-old Karen and the Anderson house in Pasadena, California.

When Dottie heard Karen's whistle, she came at once. Karen stroked Dottie's glossy, spotted coat as she snapped on her leash. She and the Dalmatian had been best friends since Dottie's arrival three years ago.

Outside, the sun was shining. With New Year's Day only two days away, everyone was looking forward to the Rose Parade. The float builders were working night and day. Karen led Dottie past a barn where many people were covering floats with beautiful flowers.

Dottie was full of energy, as always. When Karen looked into the barn, the dog barked excitedly. Karen told her to sit, and Dottie obeyed at once. A worried-looking man glanced at them. A smile replaced his frown. He turned to his friend.

"Frank," the man said, "the answer to our

Today, Dalmatians are one of the 30 most popular breeds in the United States.

5

problem is sitting on our doorstep."

The second man walked over to Karen. "I'm Frank Waverly, and that's my company's float over there," he said. "As you can see, we're creating an 1890s fire wagon. We've got a team of giant Clydesdale horses to pull it. The problem is, what's a fire wagon without a firehouse dog? We had a Dalmatian lined up, but she can't make it. Her pups came a week early."

"Do you want Dottie to ride on the float?" Karen asked.

"That's right," Frank said. "That is, if she knows how to behave around horses and doesn't mind crowds and noise."

"Dalmatians love horses," Karen told him. "She won't cause any trouble if I'm with her."

On New Year's morning, Karen was up before daylight. After a quick breakfast, she gave Dottie's coat a final brushing. When they reached the assembly area, Frank was waiting. Karen and Dottie climbed up on the driver's seat. Frank was wearing an old-time firefighter's outfit. With a smile, he put a fire helmet on Karen's head, too. Just after 8:30, the float moved into position for the parade down Colorado Boulevard.

Everyone clapped when they saw the spotted dog and the great horses. Then came a

Before a parade, a Dalmatian poses proudly on a fire truck.

6

moment when Karen's heart almost stopped. Before she could grab her, Dottie jumped off the wagon! Barking loudly, she chased off a dog that was worrying the horses. Then, still on guard duty, she trotted beside the Clydesdales.

"Now, that's a true firehouse dog," Frank said, laughing.

Karen enjoyed every minute of the morning. All too soon, the float reached the end of the parade route. "You and Dottie saved the day," Frank told Karen. "Thanks to you two, our fire wagon float looked perfect."

"You're wonderful!" Karen said to Dottie as they walked home. "Where did you come from?" As usual, Dottie didn't answer. "Well, since you won't talk, I'll have to find out for myself," Karen said with a smile.

THE HISTORY OF A SPECIAL BREED

Like all other dogs, Dalmatians are meat-eating mammals. They belong to the scientific order *Carnivora*. Dogs, jackals, wolves, and foxes are in the family known as the *Canidae*. Every domestic dog, large or small, is known by the same species name, *Canis familiaris*.

No one knows when or where Dalmatians were first *bred*. Some guess the breed was developed in a region of Yugoslavia called Dalmatia. The name fits, but the breed has never been common in that area. Another theory says the dogs were named for the Serbian poet, Jurij Dalmatin. The records show Dalmatin did raise black-and-white spotted dogs in the mid-1500s.

Still, the Dalmatian's family tree is unclear. One ancestor may have been the Talbot, a British dog used to guard a train of pack animals. Talbots, in turn, were *crossbred* with Spanish hunting dogs. Other possible ancestors include the spotted Bengal hound from India, the Harlequin Great Dane, and the Istrian hound of Yugoslavia. Another belief says Dalmatians were developed by wandering gypsies.

We do know Dalmatians have been around for at least 600 years. The breed appears in an Italian wall painting dating from about 1360 A.D. The painting presents the Dalmatian as a symbol of the Christian church. Next, Dalmatians show up in an English oil painting from the early 1600s. In the Americas, Dalmatians can be seen on a 16th-century church wall in Peru.

The name Dalmatian wasn't used in the English language until 1780. At that time, people also called the breed the plum pudding dog, spotted Dick, and the English *coach dog*. Dalmatians became famous as coach dogs when rich people trained them to trot beside their carriages. If stray dogs ran after the horses, the Dalmatians drove them off. Dalmatians also were successful as sheepdogs, hunting dogs, and rat catchers.

In the United States, Dalmatians were popular as firehouse dogs. Whenever the firebell rang, a Dalmatian led the horse-drawn fire wagon through the busy streets. When fire trucks took over, some people thought the breed might die out. Instead, the Dalmatian was adopted as a house dog. In 1959, people who saw the Disney film *101 Dalmatians* fell in love with the breed all over again. Today, Dalmatians are one of the 30 most popular breeds in the United States.

An adult male Dalmatian stands 19 to 23 inches high and weighs about 55 pounds.

THE DALMATIAN IN CLOSE-UP

A full-grown Dalmatian is a strongly built, medium-size dog. It stands 19 to 23 inches high at the *withers* (the top of the shoulder). The measurement from chest to rump is about the same. The long tail adds another 11 inches. A male dog weighs about 55 pounds, while females weigh in at 50 pounds. The American Kennel Club will not accept dogs for

The largest spots on a Dalmatian appear on its body. Smaller spots are on the head, legs, and tail.

judging that are taller than 24 inches.

A healthy Dalmatian's hair is short, hard, thick, and glossy. The dark spots, however, give the breed its special look. Spots may be either black or brown, ranging from dime-size to half-dollar-size. The largest spots appear on the body, with smaller spots on the head, legs, and tail. The spots on the body and legs of a *show dog* should never run together to make patches.

The dog's eyes and nose are usually the same color as the spots. A few Dalmatians have blue eyes or one blue eye and one brown one. Some people say blue-eyed Dalmatians are good luck. That may be, but they can't be entered in dog shows.

The Dalmatian looks alert and fit. Its head is of medium length, neither too long nor too round. The top of its skull is flat and broad between the floppy ears. Each ear tapers to a rounded point and is carried close to the head. The old practice of *cropping* a Dalmatian's ears to make them stand up has gone out of style. Unlike loose-skinned dogs, a Dalmatian's skin fits without a wrinkle. Even the dog's lips fit closely to its jaw.

The Dalmatian's teeth are those of a *carnivore*. After the baby teeth start falling out in the fifth month, its 42 adult teeth come in. The Dalmatian has three types of teeth. The upper jaw contains six *incisors* (for cutting and biting) and two *canines* (for tearing and ripping). Behind these are 12 *molars* and *premolars* (for chewing and grinding). The lower jaw has the same number of teeth in front, but has two extra molars. If properly fed, Dalmatians seldom develop cavities.

When given a meaty bone, a Dalmatian tears off big chunks with its incisors and canines. Then it turns its head to the side and works on the meat with its sharp molars. As soon as a bite is small enough to swallow, down it goes! In the stomach, strong acids begin the job of turning fats and protein into energy.

The Dalmatian's neck arches gracefully. When running, it holds its head at shoulder level. The tail serves as a rudder for balance when turning. The dog's *forelegs* are straight, with the upper joint (the elbow) close to the body. The muscular hind legs are set at right angles to the ground. This "design" gives the Dalmatian the speed it needs to keep pace with a running horse.

With its sleek, muscular hind legs, a Dalmatian can easily keep up with a running horse.

If you watch a Dalmatian, you'll see it has three *gaits*. When it's walking slowly, only one foot leaves the ground at a time. In a trot, the right-front and left-rear feet move together, followed by the left-front and right-rear feet. At full speed, the pattern changes. The dog begins to gallop by springing forward off its hind legs. When the forelegs hit, the dog bounds forward again. Meanwhile, the hind legs are swinging forward, ready for the next sprint. A gallop is really a series of high-speed jumps.

Many owners think of their Dalmatians as "almost human." To truly understand a Dalmatian, however, keep in mind that a dog's brain and senses don't operate the way a human's do.

THE DALMATIAN'S SENSES

Which animal is the smartest? Scientists say animals with larger brains tend to be the brightest. Humans, with their three-pound brains, are at the top of the list.

Dalmatians, however, learn quickly, as any trainer can tell you. But they reach their limits quickly, too. After all, an adult dog's brain weighs only two and a half ounces. With a brain that small, the dog is not capable of high-level thinking.

Here's an experiment to prove that point. If a gate has a simple latch, a Dalmatian can learn to let itself out of its pen. Once it learns the trick, it can escape whenever it's bored. But if the gate is moved to the other side of the pen, things change. The latch is still in plain sight, but the dog always goes back to the old spot. It tries and tries to open a latch that's no longer there. It cannot understand the change.

The Dalmatian's eyes also differ from a human's eyes in many ways. One difference is a third eyelid, called the *haw*. The haw is located at the corner of a dog's eye. Dalmatians are color-blind, but they see a wider field of vision than humans do. In addition, dogs see things moving better than people do. In the wild, reacting to a movement could be the difference between eating and going hungry.

A dog's ears and nose are much sharper than its senses of taste and touch. A Dalmatian can hear higher-pitched and fainter sounds than people can. Humans can't hear sounds above 20,000 cycles a second. Dogs hear sounds in the 30,000-cycle range and above. That's why people can't hear a "soundless" dog whistle, but a dog can. In another test, a scientist dropped a steel ball onto a metal plate. Humans could hear the click of the ball up to 20 feet away. A Dalmatian, with its sharper ears, heard the tiny click at 80 feet away.

The Dalmatian's sense of smell leaves a human's even farther behind. The ability to detect odors begins with the *olfactory patches* in the nose. Unless a human breathes hard, these patches don't send much of a message to the brain. Dogs have a much larger olfactory area. Every breath they take opens up a world of smells humans can't even imagine. Trained dogs, for example, are used to patrol airports and harbors. These animals are able to sniff out drugs hidden in suitcases and other packages.

Dalmatians show off their keen sense of smell almost every day. They identify their own family by their body odors. If you have touched a baseball bat, your dog can pick that bat out of a hundred others. Of course, dogs like some odors better than others. The smell of meat makes them wild with joy, but the scent of fear on a stranger brings out aggressive behavior. Just like humans, each Dalmatian has its own personality.

A DOG WITH REAL CHARACTER

The time is the 1700s. Imagine a golden coach, drawn by a team of matching horses. Two spotted dogs trot beside the horses as they canter down a country lane. When dogs run out and try to spook the horses, the Dalmatians chase them away. The Dalmatians are not afraid of bandits, either. Seeing the dogs on guard, most bandits wait for easier prey.

This description gives you a good idea of the Dalmatian's character. As a breed, these dogs are fearless, hard workers. Once they're properly trained, they'll try hard to please their owners. In public, they're calm and easy to handle. When a stranger stops to talk, they accept the newcomer if their owner says it's okay. Some owners swear their Dalmatians grin when they're happy. To a stranger, that grin may look like a snarl. With its sharp

Once a Dalmatian is properly trained, it will try hard to please its owner.

teeth showing, a Dalmatian can look quite mean.

The Dalmatian likes to hunt, but most hunters prefer other breeds. As a result, Dalmatians are usually family pets. The qualities that made them good coach dogs and firehouse dogs make them good pets, as well. They guard their family and its property without being mean. Clean and sturdy, they are seldom ill. If there are children in the family, the Dalmatian enjoys playing with them.

For all their good qualities, Dalmatians aren't for everyone. Shut up in an apartment, a bored Dalmatian can do a great deal of damage. Dalmatians need owners who can give them enough exercise.

Dalmatians also need owners who will take the time to train them. They're eager to learn, but they can't be pushed too fast. Along with basic obedience training, they seem to enjoy performing tricks. Circus clowns know this and often use Dalmatians in their acts.

Owners say their Dalmatians are alert and dependable. Except for their constant *shedding*, they're easy to care for. Instead of loving only one person, they love everyone in their human families. Unlike some breeds, Dalmatians don't grieve when separated from their owners. If another family adopts one, it settles down quickly in its new home.

After you meet your first Dalmatian, you may want one of your own. Most people decide to buy their first Dalmatian when it's still a *puppy*.

Healthy Dalmatian puppies should not be too shy or too aggressive. The best puppies are alert, playful, and clean.

CHOOSING A DALMATIAN PUPPY

Many people have questions about what to look for when they're buying a Dalmatian puppy. How old should the puppy be? Should it be skinny or fat? Aggressive or calm?

Here are the most popular questions asked by buyers and the experts' answers:

Should Dalmatians be bought from a pet store or a breeder? If you buy from a breeder,

you'll be able to see the puppy's mother. That will give you an idea of what the grown-up puppy will be like. Best of all, you can pick your puppy from one or more *litters*. A pet store, on the other hand, may have only one puppy to show you. To make up for that, most pet stores will guarantee the health of the puppy. Small-time breeders who sell only a few puppies don't always guarantee their dogs. You can get a list of good breeders and pet stores from your local *veterinarian* or animal hospital.

How should a healthy puppy look and act? A healthy puppy will be alert, playful, and clean. Don't worry if the pup's spots look too large. The puppy will grow into them. Never buy a puppy that has cloudy eyes, a swollen belly, or a runny nose. Reject any Dalmatian that fails a hearing test. Do not buy a puppy that is too shy or too aggressive, either. Ask the seller for the puppy's health record, including its shots. Once you buy your dog, take it to a vet for an exam. If the dog fails the checkup, return it to the seller.

Can Dalmatians be show dogs? Your Dalmatian can be both a pet and a show dog. Show dogs, however, must meet the standards set for the breed. If you want a show dog, ask someone who knows about Dalmatians to help

Before buying a Dalmatian, look at the puppy's mother. The mother can give you an idea of what the puppy will look like and how it will act when it is older.

you make your choice. Expect to pay from $300 to $450 for a pet-quality Dalmatian. A show-quality dog will cost $450 and up.

Is it important that a Dalmatian be a purebred? A *purebred* dog carries the qualities of its breed. No one can predict what crossbred puppies will be like. To be sure your puppy is a purebred, ask for its "papers." The seller will give you the puppy's *pedigree.* The pedigree is a list of the dog's male and female ancestors.

Send the pedigree and your bill of sale to one of the national kennel clubs. This protects the value of your Dalmatian's pups if you decide to breed it. Show dogs should also be registered.

Should I buy a male or a female puppy? If you plan to raise puppies, you'll want to buy a female. If not, a male puppy is usually a little cheaper. Both male and female Dalmatians make good pets. A male dog won't roam if he is well trained and your yard is properly fenced in. Females present a different kind of problem. Twice a year, a female is ready to mate and have puppies. This is known as coming into *heat*. Male dogs will be attracted to her, and they must be kept away if you do not want her to have puppies.

How old should a puppy be? A Dalmatian pup is ready to go home with you when it's 49 days old. Younger puppies still need their mothers and the company of their litter mates. Older dogs can be equally good pets. For one thing, you know at once what the dog will look like and how it will behave. If you don't want to do all the training yourself, buying an older dog might be the answer. Training a puppy takes time and patience.

Older Dalmatians make good pets because they are already trained.

TRAINING YOUR DALMATIAN

Once you take a puppy home, the fun begins. A puppy used to being handled will soon adjust to its new home. People sometimes forget, however, that dogs are dogs. They are born with many of the impulses of wild pack animals. They instinctively want to mark their territory. If you don't want your Dalmatian to wreck your house, you must train it.

The first goal is to *housebreak* your dog. No one wants a puppy that leaves messes around the house. Luckily, Dalmatians won't soil their own sleeping places. The problem begins when the puppy uses the indoor carpet instead of the outdoor grass. You must be the teacher.

The first step is to put your puppy on a regular schedule. You'll see it usually relieves itself after eating. Your job is to feed it at the same time every day. Then take it outside to the spot you want it to use. The odors it leaves there will encourage it to use the spot again.

But puppies make mistakes. When that happens, speak sharply to your dog. Hold its nose close to the mess while you scold it. Then take it outside. Afterward, wash the area with a strong cleaner. Remove any odor that might lead to more use of the spot. When the puppy performs correctly, pet it. Say, "Good dog, that's a good puppy!" If you do this, your puppy will work hard to earn more praise.

If you're patient and consistent, your puppy will learn quickly. Always use your dog's name when you talk to it. Say, for example, "Down, Pepper!" when he jumps up on you. When he obeys, praise him. You can make him work harder by giving him a dog biscuit. Rewarding your dog is known as *reinforcing* the good behavior. A hungry puppy will do almost anything for a treat.

Dalmatians need exercise, which means going for many walks. When you leave the yard, put your puppy on a lead. At 12 weeks, your puppy should have a *choke chain*. That sounds cruel, but it's kinder than a regular collar. Buy a chain with thick links. When you go outdoors, the eager puppy will try to run away. Jerk back on the chain and say, "Stay!" Loosen the chain at the same time. Walk at a steady pace, dragging your puppy with you, if necessary. Remember to praise it when it walks at your side. In a week or two, your puppy will be a well-behaved walking companion.

Another important command is "Come." Teach your puppy this command by the time it's three months old. Start by tying a 30-foot rope to its collar. Let it roam until it finds something exciting. Then say, "Come!" in a firm voice. Reward your dog if it obeys. If it doesn't, repeat the command as you give the rope a sharp jerk. Repeat the process three or four times during a training session.

Each new command your puppy learns makes it easier to teach it new ones. A well-trained dog also needs to know how to sit, stay, and heel on command. "To heel" means the dog takes up a position just behind your left foot. Once a Dalmatian masters these commands, it will never forget them.

CARING FOR YOUR DALMATIAN

Having a Dalmatian as a pet adds joy to any owner's life. The fun has a price, however. Dogs need proper care. To most people that means feeding and housing their pets. A loving owner knows care also means *grooming,* visiting the vet, and exercising.

Just like humans, Dalmatians must have a balanced diet. They need protein, fat, and starch—but not in the same amounts you do. The easiest way to feed your new puppy is to give it canned dog food and puppy meal. If you add cows' milk, the puppy will have a balanced diet. Some owners prefer to feed their puppy ground beef, cow's milk, and brown bread.

The size and number of meals is important. A puppy needs about one-half ounce of food for each pound of body weight. An eight-week-old puppy needs to be fed five times a day. When it is four months, reduce the meals to three. Cut down to two meals a day when it is nine months. A dog leaves puppyhood when it's a year old. Adult dogs need about 24 ounces of raw meat and cereals a day. Feed a full-grown dog once or twice a day. If you feed it only at night, give the dog a few biscuits in the morning.

What you *don't* feed your dog is also important. Never give fish or chicken bones to your Dalmatian. If a small bone sticks in the dog's throat, it will choke to death. Candy is another no-no. Dogs love sweets, but candy will cause cavities and has little food value. Finally, don't feed your dog from the table. If you never start, the dog will never learn to beg.

Dalmatians adjust to any climate, so they're easy to house. Give an indoor dog a dog bed lined with newspapers and a blanket. An outdoor dog needs a dry, sturdy doghouse. The doghouse should be large enough for the dog to stretch in. Fix up a raised bed inside the doghouse so the dog can sleep off the ground. Always keep a dish of fresh water close by.

Grooming your Dalmatian twice a week will keep it sleek and clean. Brushing removes burrs and tones the skin. Brushing also cuts down on the dog hair that gets shed in the house. Dalmatians love to be brushed, but bathe them only when they're dirty. Always rinse the dog fully and dry it with a fluffy towel. A wet dog always shakes itself, so you might want to wear old clothes!

A healthy Dalmatian starts life with a series of "puppy shots." These protect the dog from *distemper* and other serious diseases. For older dogs, the most common problems are fleas and *worms*. Shampoos, flea powders, and flea collars should take care of biting pests. Fleas breed in your dog's bed, so keep that area clean. The signs of worms include a potbelly, runny eyes, and vomiting. You also may see worms in the dog's droppings. Take your

Dalmatians love to play fetch-the-stick — although sometimes they don't like to give up the stick.

dog to the vet at once. Worming a dog, like treating any serious illness, is a job for an expert.

A healthy dog needs exercise. Play a game of fetch-the-stick. Go for a fast walk. Make up games together. Running on a hard surface will keep the dog's claws worn down. Remember, you bought a Dalmatian because it's a "people dog." The time you spend together will be good for both of you.

BREEDING YOUR DALMATIAN

If you have a female Dalmatian, you're certain to think about breeding her. Puppies are such fun! Also, you might make some money by selling the puppies. But breeding a Dalmatian *bitch,* an adult female dog, isn't a simple matter.

First, think about the age and health of your dog. If she is over four years old, she may be too old for a first litter. Ask your vet for advice. A young dog shouldn't be bred the first time she comes into heat. You'll also want your pet to be in tip-top shape. If she's too fat, for example, wait until she's lost some weight. Finally, never breed a dog that's bad tempered, too shy, or too nervous. The puppies may inherit these qualities.

The next step is to find a *stud.* Most Dalmatian kennels have a champion male they use for breeding. You can find the kennels' addresses in dog magazines or in classified ads. If possible, visit a kennel. Make sure the male is good tempered and healthy. Some stud services will check your female as well. They want to be sure she's free of defects. Careful breeders try to make sure all puppies are perfect when they're born.

Count the days from the time your bitch comes into heat. The best time for breeding is between the eleventh and fifteenth days. Take her to the stud for the mating. With luck, your dog will become pregnant. If she does not, the owner of the stud should let you bring her back once again.

You can pay the stud fee in two ways. If you hope to produce a champion show dog, pay the fee in cash. Otherwise, the stud's owner will take the "pick of the litter." You save money, but you give up your best puppy. A kennel owner who likes the looks of a bitch also may ask for "first refusal." When you sell the puppies, the kennel has the right to buy the one it wants.

Once the female has mated, keep her away from other males until she's out of heat. If she mates again, she may give birth to puppies from both males. If she is pregnant, you'll see her body getting heavier. Let your vet check her to be sure all is well. A pregnant bitch needs more protein and less starch. Milk and eggs are good additions to her diet. Give her plenty of gentle exercise, but try to keep her from jumping. As the time for birth comes near, fix up a box for her *whelping* (the birth). In a normal birth, the dog will take care of the rest.

Breeding your dog can be expensive. You may have to pay a stud fee. The vet will charge for checking the female and for giving the puppies their shots. Later on, you'll have to feed and house the puppies until they're sold. If all of them sell quickly, you'll be a winner. That doesn't always happen, however. The cost of feeding three or four half-grown Dalmatians can quickly add up.

Breeders will tell you they raise Dalmatians for love, not profit. Most of them are happy to break even. By all means, breed your female. But don't expect to get rich.

THE BIRTH OF A DALMATIAN

Nothing excites a Dalmatian's owner more than the arrival of a new litter.

A Dalmatian female carries her puppies for about nine weeks. Litters of 10 or more puppies are quite common. The record belongs to a bitch who gave birth to 17 puppies!

After all the puppies in her litter are born, the female nudges the puppies close and nurses them.

Each newborn puppy, or *whelp*, emerges headfirst. The mother helps the pup out of the birth sac and licks the pup until it starts breathing. Then she bites through the *umbilical cord*. With that job done, she licks the blind, squirming pup to clean, warm, and comfort it. The next pup appears about 30 minutes later.

The newborn puppies are almost helpless. The female nudges them into position to start feeding. The touch and smell of her *teats* starts them nursing.

A newborn Dalmatian puppy is pure white. Only the faintest of Dalmatian spots are showing. The real spots show up in about three weeks.

If all goes well, the puppies grow rapidly. At 21 days, their eyes open and they are able to hear. Chubby and awkward, the pups scramble around on unsteady legs. They can wag their tails and bark when they want to nurse.

The female doesn't always give in to the puppies' demands. By the time the puppies are 21 days old, the mother is ready to *wean* them, or make them stop nursing. You can help by letting the puppies suck a milk-and-

broth mixture from your finger. Before long, the pups will be able to lap milk from a pan. By four weeks, the pups should be eating four small meals a day from a bowl. The puppies will be cutting their baby teeth and can chew soft puppy food. The mother will let them nurse only at night. By six weeks, they should be totally weaned.

When the puppies are about 21 days old, the owner should test each pup's hearing. An average of one in eight Dalmatian puppies is born deaf. Those that can't hear must be taken to the vet and put to sleep. Putting a dog to sleep may sound cruel, but deaf dogs don't make good pets. Because they can't hear, they often become biters. In addition, deaf dogs are helpless in traffic.

By the eighth week, the healthy puppies are ready to go to new homes. Leggy and full of mischief, they're well on their way to becoming full-grown Dalmatians.

When Dalmatian puppies are 21 days old, their spots appear and their eyes open.

WHY DOES A DALMATIAN WAG ITS TAIL?

Johnny Woods is the proud owner of a young Dalmatian. When Johnny comes home from school, Dally is waiting to greet him. With a woof, the dog jumps into Johnny's arms and licks his face. At the same time, Dally's tail wags back and forth.

Johnny wonders, "Why does my dog wag her tail? Perhaps she's happy to see me, and tail wagging is her way of showing she loves me."

Johnny's only half right. When Dally whips her tail back and forth, she *is* being friendly. But, that's not all she's telling him. Mixed in with the happiness is a measure of fear. After all, Johnny is the leader of Dally's pack! He's bigger and stronger than she is. She loves him, but she also fears him. She knows she must do what he says.

"Wait a minute," Johnny protests. "I love my dog. She doesn't have any reason to be afraid of me."

Most dog owners would agree with Johnny.

They don't like to think their dogs fear them. But think about dogs and humans for a moment. Dally depends upon Johnny for her survival. He feeds her, grooms her, and plays with her. She has learned to obey him. Remember, dogs don't think like humans. Their behavior is driven by *instinct,* not by reason.

Newborn Dalmatian puppies don't wag their tails. The first tail wagging appears in the third week. After that, if you watch the pups feeding, you'll see their tails wagging. "Isn't that cute?" you say to yourself. "They're so happy to be feeding together."

Dog experts have a different view of what this means. They say tail wagging starts when puppies begin rough-and-tumble play. The stronger pups bully the weaker ones. Everyone gets chased and nipped. Then, feeding time comes. The pups are hungry, but they're also fearful of each other. As they crowd in to suckle, instinct drives them to wag their tails. The wagging eases the tension and lets them get on with feeding.

As the puppies grow up, tail wagging also serves as a message to other dogs. Watch two dogs from the same kennel when they meet. As they circle one another, each wags its tail. The "top" dog, the one who is dominant, holds its tail high. The tail moves in stiff, short

To relieve tension, Dalmatian puppies often wag their tails while eating.

strokes. The other dog's tail droops lower. The tail wags in long, loose strokes. The message is clear: "I'm glad to see you, but I'm also a little worried. Is everything okay?"

Finally, tail wagging has one more purpose. A wagging tail "broadcasts" the dog's personal scent. These scents are produced by anal glands under the tail. As the tail wags, it squeezes the glands. The faint odors don't mean anything to humans. To dogs, it's their way of recognizing a friend.

What does all this mean to Johnny? When he comes home from school, he'll see Dally's tail wagging for what it is. He won't let her forget her training, but he'll give her a loving pat and a kind word. Both owner and dog will feel good about their friendship.

BESSIE, THE FIREHOUSE DOG

The year is 1910. The city is New York. Suddenly, the alarm sounds at Engine Company No. 30. Firefighters pull on their boots and heavy coats. One by one, they slide down the brass pole. Quickly, the men harness the waiting horses. Black smoke pours from the boilers on the pump wagon. With a great clatter, the wagon pulls out into the crowded street. Running ahead to clear the way is Bessie, the firehouse Dalmatian.

Bessie is the mascot of the station. Captain Joseph Donovan, a Dalmatian breeder, gave her to the company. Lt. Wise takes care of Bessie. He says he didn't have to train her.

When the alarm bell rings, Bessie knows what to do. Forty times a month, for almost six years, she does her job.

The station is located at the corner of Third Avenue and 67th Street. Horse-drawn carriages, bicycles, and people are everywhere. When the alarm clangs, Bessie springs into action. Her barking echoes down the street. People on foot, wagon drivers, and streetcar motormen stop when they hear her. The station's three white horses follow the swift, spotted dog. When they reach the fire, Bessie

In the United States during the late 1800s and early 1900s, Dalmatians were most often seen at fire stations.

follows the firefighters into the building. She knows the rules and the risks. She always stays one floor below the firefighters. If the men have to make a sudden retreat, they won't stumble over her.

Bessie is well known in the city. She follows Lt. Wise when he takes the streetcar home. Usually, the conductors won't let dogs into the cars. Bessie is special. She wears a brass fire helmet on her collar. The helmet marks her as a fire department dog, and she rides for free. Lt. Wise reports that Bessie knows the route as well as he does. If he's not there, she travels back and forth by herself.

But Bessie's exciting life is coming to an end. Ever since 1892, motor vehicles have been taking over the streets. Now, without warning, a fire engine has replaced the station's horses. Bessie is confused, but she does her best. At the next alarm, she leads the engine as far as Third Avenue. Then she tucks her tail between her legs and returns to the station house. She never runs to another fire.

Bessie has two last moments of fame. In 1910, she competes in a dog show at Madison Square Garden. Lt. Wise enters her in a special class for fire station Dalmatians. Bessie wins second place, behind a male named Mike. Six years later, author Kate Sanborn talks to

Lt. Wise about Bessie. As they talk, Bessie puts her head in Lt. Wise's hand. Wise swears she knows they're talking about her.

Bessie is gone, but Dalmatians still live in firehouses. Many firefighters keep them as good-luck mascots. Other Dalmatians are groomed and trained carefully for dog shows. Still others enjoy quieter lives as family pets. Dalmatians, with their bright coats and black spots, make any owner proud.

Some Dalmatians are kept by firefighters as mascots, and others are groomed and trained as show dogs. Most Dalmatians enjoy quiet lives as pets.

▉ GLOSSARY/INDEX

GLOSSARY/INDEX

■GLOSSARY/INDEX